Mrs Kirkham.

J. M. Dent & Sons Limited London

First published 1973

First published by the School Journal,
Department of Education, New Zealand
Reproduction by
Iberico Fotomecanica, Madrid
Printed in Great Britain by
London Litho Ltd.
ISBN 0 460 05860 6

The Railway Engine and the Hairy Brigands

story by

Margaret Mahy

pictures by

Brian Froud

1 What happened first

There was once a rich man who decided he wasn't getting the best out of life, so . . . he decided to run away to sea.

"But before I go," he said, "I will sell all my goods and give to the poor." Which he did. But, when everything else was sold, something was left on a siding behind his house—an old railway engine which nobody, not even the poor, wanted.

"I shall give that to my relatives," said the rich man. The relatives, who had watched sourly while the rich man gave to the poor, said they did not want it.

"Well, it's all I've got left," the rich man said. "I suppose I'll have to send it to the scrap yard."

But . . . "Wait!" called a voice and the smallest relatives of all came through the legs of the other relatives. The smallest relatives were Penelope and her sister little Bridget.

"I'll take the railway engine," said Penny. "I will look after it while you are at sea."

"My dear, we haven't got any coal for it," said Penny's mother.

"Well," said the rich man's lawyer who was standing there looking miserable. "I find the rich man still has a coal mine which hasn't been given to the poor."

"Good, good!" said the rich man. "Give the coal mine and steam engine to Penny and little Bridget. Now I am going to sea."

The rich man went to sea and spent many happy years there until he was eaten by sharks while skin diving in the Bahamas. It is only fair to mention that the sharks thought he was someone else. They might have eaten him anyway, but we must give them the benefit of the doubt.

2 The Railway Engine annoys Mr Samuel Heratick

Penny and little Bridget took the railway engine home with them. "Steam engines are much more fun than diesel ones," said Penny. She piled its cooker full of coal. *SSSSSSSSSSSSSSSS* went the engine as the furnace burned, the water turned to steam and the steam made the wheels go around. Off they went, Penny and little Bridget taking turns to be the driver, both looking clever and thoughtful.

The steam engine went down the main street of town and all the people of that town said:

"Well, *some* folk know how to enjoy themselves I *must* say!"

And all the little boys in that town and all the dogs too, chased after the steam engine. The boys yelled and the dogs barked, or sometimes for a change the dogs yelled and the boys barked, but either way all was noise *noise* NOISE, especially when Penny and little Bridget whistled the whistle, and all the drivers of all the cars in that town tooted their horns.

At the door of his shop a snappy old man stood, watching. "Bah!" he said, not sadly like a sheep but sharply like a shotgun. "Those girls will bewilder and bewitch us with hootings and screechings until we are dormouse-deaf and our ears will be no use to us at all. They'll be mere ornamental curlicues on either side of our heads.

"Bah!" he said again. "Those lackadaisical girls and their lethal locomotive will set fire to all this town. We'll be cooked to cinders in our beds, flames will leap up as twirly and bright as devil's whiskers and they'll twist around us, serpent-sharp, and eat us down to black and grinning bones."

But this man (he was nobody's uncle and his name was Mr Samuel Heratick) was wrong. As you will see!

Every day Penelope and little Bridget drove their steam engine three times around the town. They taught it to laugh like a kookaburra bird and to cackle like a witch. Not everybody liked this, mind you. Mr S. Heratick did not like it at all, but there is no pleasing some people.

"Cackle! Cackle!" he muttered as they went by. "You'd think that that there steam engine had laid an egg. Hoot! Hoot! You'd swear we'd been invaded by an army of owls."

He went back into his shop in disgust.

G.R.

3 The invasion of the Hairy Brigands

Mr S. Heratick's shop was called "The Wet-Weather Shop" and sold gumboots and raincoats, galoshes and umbrellas both plain and striped. However, he did not do very well because it scarcely ever rained in that town and when it did everyone wanted to paddle in the puddles not guard their feet with gumboots. This made Mr S. Heratick very bitter and gave him the idea that things were against him. Up in the hills it rained all the time, but it was no use Mr S. Heratick setting up shop there because the only people who lived in the hills were the Hairy Brigands. Now, as everyone knows, a Hairy Brigand will snitch and snatch gumboots, but he won't buy them, ever, ever, ever. No wonder Mr S. Heratick hated people enjoying themselves with steam engines and such like. I would be like that too, if I had a wet-weather shop in a dry-weather town.

But Mr S. Heratick shouldn't have been quite so cross with things as they were then, because the next week they got worse: that town was invaded and quite taken over by brigands. Down from the hills came the Hairy Brigands themselves—all of them—and they were quite horrible to see. Through spending all their lives in the

S. HERATICK
The WETWEATHER SHOP

rain they had grown hair between their fingers and toes and squelched like water-logged socks as they came skirmishing along. They had red hair all over them and even their ears were hairy round the edges. (They had grown this hair to stop water getting in their ears.)

Their pockets were filled with gold and silver fish, and flipperty-gibbet, green freckled frogs.

Such was the hideous aspect of the Hairy Brigands of the hills.

All the people in that town hid because they did not wish to have anything to do with the Hairy Brigands. Who would protect that town? The policeman hid, and the traffic cop, and the mayor and the council hid, and the public accountant and the lawyer and the bank manager. In fact all the important people in town hid and so did all the unimportant ones. When the Hairy Brigands marched into the main street of that town the only person they could see was Mr Heratick trying desperately to lock and block his

Wet-Weather Shop against them. But all in vain! The Hairy Brigands seized him furiously and charged at his shop with delight.

"Umbrellas!" they cried. "Just what we always wanted. Gumboots—all sizes of largeness! Galoshes—all sizes of smallness. Raincoats—all rubberized, plasticated, waterproofed and striped like rainbows. Just what we've always needed."

While Mr S. Heratick wrung his hands, the Hairy Brigands began to quarrel over who was to have the raincoats with the hoods and all was chaos.

Mr S. Heratick was helpless, unable to save his shop. He was nearly torn in two by despair and desolation.

Then like the trumpet of an approaching army came a sound on the sunny air—a shrill clear cry and shouting and barking and the running of many feet. The Brigands cocked their hairy ears—pricked them forward like cat's ears, a thing they had learned to do up in the damp and dripping hills. They drew their swords and gnashed their teeth and flourished their umbrellas, presenting a generally ferocious aspect.

But their ferocity changed to terrified whimpering as a great monster swept around the corner, followed by all the dogs and all the little boys in that town. You and I would have known it was the Steam Engine driven by Penelope and little Bridget, but the Hairy Brigands were ignorant as well as hairy and did not know what was what! They had never seen a steam engine before. Not only that, Penny, little Bridget, and all the boys and all the dogs in that town had painted a terrible face on the front of the engine. It looked most fearsome chuffling and steaming along.

It happened that the chief of the Hairy Brigands could read, and on long wet evenings in the hills he would get out his book of fairy tales and read to his brigands tales of witches and goblins. So the brigands knew everything about witches—everything except what they looked like. When Penelope made the steam engine cackle like a witch they thought the steam engine *was* a witch.

TO THE
HILLS

When she made it laugh like a kookaburra they *still* thought it was a witch, except for one bird-loving brigand, who shouted "That's a kookaburra!" Fortunately all the other Brigands were shouting "That's a witch!" so loudly that they did not hear the bird-lover.

Consumed with terror the Hairy Brigands dropped their bright raincoats, the umbrellas, the galoshes and even the gumboots, and fled back towards the dim and misty shadow of the rainy hills.

4 What happened after that

Out of hiding came the policeman, the traffic cop, the mayor and the council. Out of hiding came the doctor, the lawyer, the public accountant and the bank manager. Out came all the people of that town, both the important and unimportant. But no boys—big and little—came out of hiding—and no dogs, for they were already out, some dancing around the railway engine and some trying on the gumboots that belonged to Mr S. Heratick.

Mr S. Heratick himself was running madly here and there, collecting the gumboots which lay scattered around before any boys or dogs could get to them. But nobody took any notice of him. Everyone was making speeches praising the railway engine and the splendid courage and cleverness of Penny and little Bridget and all the boys and all the dogs of that town.

The mayor said he would get golden medals made for all of them, and the doctor offered to listen to their hearts for nothing.

CHEAP

No treat was considered too wonderful for them. A great party was started for them straight away. Tables were set up around the steam engine. The mayor and the council blew up two thousand balloons and let them loose among the children. The food shops gave cakes and jellies and ice creams and sausage rolls and all was enormous fun and games.

Then suddenly it began to rain, a thing which I may have told you, very, *very* seldom happened in that town. As it was, half the sun shone from behind the clouds so that the air was full of rainbows, all mixed up with the rain.

Nobody wanted to leave the party, rain or no rain, so everyone rushed into the Wet-Weather Shop and bought raincoats and umbrellas like gay cartwheels, galoshes and even gumboots. They even put an umbrella over the chimney of the railway engine to keep the rain from its fire. Mr S. Heratick, who had been sulking sourly, made enough money to last him until next time it rained.

As for Penelope and little Bridget they enjoyed the party more than anyone else, being delighted that their railwav engine should be the hero of that town.

You would think that Mr S. Heratick would love the steam engine now, seeing how it had saved his gumboots for him, but he remained the same grumbler as before.

"A pretty thing it is," he muttered, "when a man's got to depend on a tooting, hooting railway engine and two little female girls to protect his gumboots and galoshes."

(It just shows you can't change some people for the better, and even a steam engine isn't enough to reform a truly crosspatch retailer.)

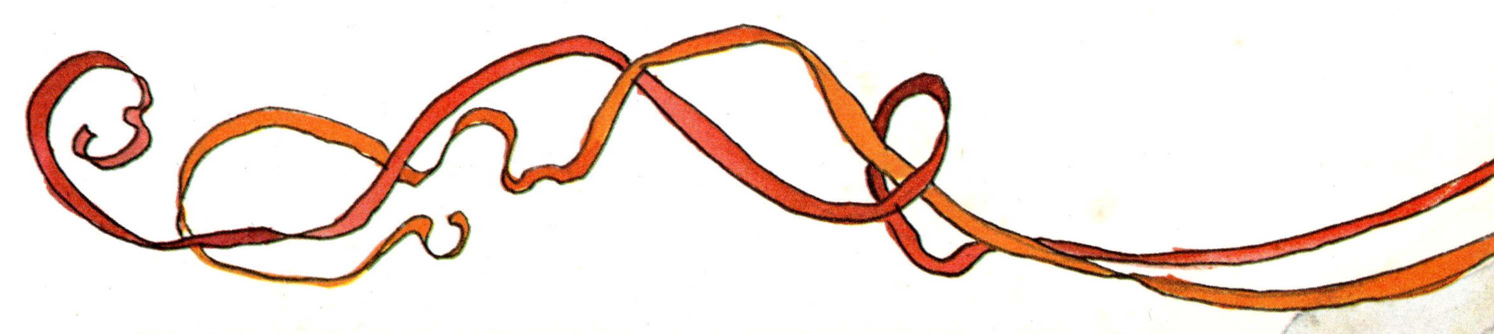

But Penelope and little Bridget drove their railway engine home that night with lots of singing and laughing which is just how all adventures should end. The sparks from their engine went up into the air so high they looked like stars . . . in fact, perhaps they did turn into stars. No one could be *sure* with an engine like that, part engine, part kookaburra, part cackling witch.

Anyhow, everyone in that town lived happily ever after, especially Penny and little Bridget, and no brigands, hairy or plain bothered them again.

5 What happened to the Hairy Brigands

Well, what *did* happen to the Hairy Brigands? They stayed in their rainy hills for ever after. They grew more hair on their ears and umbrellas out of the tops of their heads and were really quite comfortable in spite of the rain. Sometimes they would look at that town from the top of their hills and say:

"Witches live there! It is truly a town where witches live."

But, as you and I know, this was just their hairy idea of things.

C.R. MA

THE CHELSEA YEARS 1915-1923

Hunterian Art Gallery
University of Glasgow
2 July – 27 August, 1994

Heinz Gallery,
Royal Institute of British Architects,
21 Portman Square, London
8 September – 29 October, 1994

Preface and Acknowledgements

The eight years Mackintosh spent in London, from 1915 to 1923, have generally been treated as a postscript to his extraordinary career in Glasgow. In particular the architectural projects after Glasgow have received cursory attention. This exhibition and its accompanying catalogue attempt to redress the balance by focusing on the architectural work. In addition the significance of Wenman J. Bassett-Lowke, Mackintosh's major patron during the Chelsea years, is reconsidered.

The realisation of both exhibition and catalogue has depended in large part on the meticulous scholarship of the guest co-curator, Alan Crawford. He has collaborated on both the selection and scripting of the exhibition in addition to contributing to the catalogue. Janet Bassett-Lowke, W.J. Bassett-Lowke's niece, has enriched the project with her dedicated enthusiasm. We are grateful to her for the affectionate and insightful memoir of her uncle, which more than justifies his faith in her journalistic skills.

For the first time, Mackintosh's principal studio scheme from the Chelsea years has been realised in three dimensions. Preliminary research for the model was carried out by Mark Dyson, a graduate of the Mackintosh School of Architecture. Detailed evaluation of the surviving drawings and construction of the model have been undertaken by Stephen Perry, of the Gallery's technical staff. Throughout, Professor Andy MacMillan of the Mackintosh School has given freely of his advice.

The Gallery is in addition grateful to those lenders who have generously agreed loans for both venues: the Trustees of the British Museum; Strathclyde University Archives; the British Architectural Library Drawings Collection of the Royal Institute of British Architects; Northamptonshire Record Office; and Janet Bassett-Lowke.

It is highly appropriate that this exhibition should have a London venue and that that venue should be the Royal Institute of British Architects' gallery; Mackintosh's last submission of architectural drawings for exhibition, a proposal for studios in Chelsea, was to the R.I.B.A. in 1922. This exhibition will be shown at its Heinz Gallery, and is part of a continuing collaboration with the R.I.B.A. Drawings Collection which last year allowed the Hunterian to select a handsome group of Voysey's decorative designs for exhibition in Glasgow.

Pamela Robertson, Curator

LOST AND FOUND

ARCHITECTURAL PROJECTS AFTER GLASGOW

1. *A Warehouse Block in an Arcaded Street* (cat. 3)

by **ALAN CRAWFORD**

Lost and Found: Architectural Projects after Glasgow

"The one definite impression of these works subsequent to his departure from Glasgow, is of a man who has lost his way."[1]

Between 1896 and 1907 Mackintosh designed about 50 buildings and interiors, including almost all his best-known works. Between 1908 and 1914 he completed nine small jobs, none of major significance. He was drinking heavily; he was a liability in the office of Honeyman, Keppie and Mackintosh; and his financial affairs were in a mess.[2] What had gone wrong? Was he embittered by lack of recognition? Did he feel that British architecture, increasingly systematic and Classical, was passing him by? Or was he simply burned out?[3] Things came to a head in 1913 when he resigned from the partnership. In July 1914 the Mackintoshes went to Walberswick in Suffolk for their holidays. Within weeks war was declared. Margaret persuaded Mackintosh "to just stop on and get the real rest cure that he has so badly needed for quite two years."[4] She let their house in Glasgow and, so far as is known, Mackintosh never went back there. This essay looks at the architectural work which he did after Glasgow, and asks whether it is the work of a man who has lost his way.

Mackintosh took things quietly in Walberswick, and by January 1915 Margaret could write: "Already Toshie is quite a different being and evidently at the end of the year will be quite fit again..."[5] But then in May, after some local people learned that he had worked in Germany and Austria, the military authorities came and confiscated private papers. Orders to leave the area were subsequently served.[6] Mackintosh, who was fiercely patriotic, went up to London to clear his name; while he was there he did some work for Patrick Geddes, who was running a Summer Meeting on *The War: Its Social Tasks and Problems*; in July Mackintosh wrote to his friend and patron William Davidson that he was "playing around with Prof Geddes".[7]

The two elevations entitled *A Warehouse Block in an Arcaded Street* and *Shop and Office Block*

2. *Shop and Office Block in an Arcaded Street* (cat. 4)

in an Arcaded Street may belong to this episode, for they were clearly intended for a hot country, and Geddes had town-planning consultancies in India; there was even talk of Mackintosh going to work out there (ills. 1 and 2).[8] There are clear allusions to eastern architecture in these designs: the arcade of the shop and office block has Egyptian bud capitals and the two shop entrances are loosely based on the gates of the Great Stupa at Sanchi, Madhya Pradesh, in India.[9] But at the same time there are influences from Viennese architecture and design which were an abiding source of inspiration for Mackintosh in these years: the frames round the façades and the galleried attic storey on the shop and office block, recall Josef Hoffmann's Palais Stoclet of 1905-10.[10] We do not know the context of these designs, and should not judge them as if they were proposals for real buildings. They may have been made to illustrate a point for Geddes, and were scarcely a test of Mackintosh's powers of design. The eastern references are, perhaps, clumsy, but what was Mackintosh to do? He was rootless in London, trying to persuade the Home Office that he was not a spy, and designing buildings to go on the other side of the world.

Margaret joined him in August; they found adjoining studios in Glebe Place, Chelsea, and lodgings nearby.[11] And so began eight years of living in London, years of which it is now impossible to recover the emotional tone. They made friends with artists and musicians, mostly younger than themselves, and hovered on the fringes of the avant-garde. They had little money, and ate most evenings at the Blue Cockatoo, a cheap and incompetent restaurant, frequented by artists, on Cheyne Walk.[12] They were becoming, perhaps they wanted to be, Bohemians. Thomas Howarth wrote of them living quite happily and sociably, and of the popularity of Margaret's tea parties "where minute attention was paid to every detail"; but he also wrote of a young architect who went to Mackintosh looking for work, and found him so depressed that he was almost unable to speak.[13]

Soon after they settled in Chelsea, perhaps around Christmas 1915, Mackintosh was offered a job by W.J. Bassett-Lowke of Northampton. Janet Bassett-Lowke has provided a telling and affectionate portrait of her uncle for this catalogue; here it is enough to note that he was a typical early English Modernist, a man of business, machinery and imagination with a taste for the out-of-doors; and that he was, among Mackintosh's clients, far and away the most knowledgeable about architecture and design. He was in his late thirties and engaged to be married, and he wanted an architect with modern ideas to alter and enlarge an early 19th-century terraced house in Northampton for him. While he was on holiday in Cornwall in 1915, a friend from Glasgow told him about Mackintosh.[14]

78 Derngate was three storeys high over a basement and only two rooms deep, and the staircase was next to the front door, leaving a parlour only eight feet wide. Mackintosh moved the staircase through 90 degrees so that it ran across the middle of the house, making the parlour shallower but much wider (ill. 3). On the published plans the parlour was renamed the lounge-hall, and Mackintosh provided somewhere to sit by adding a single-storey bay window to the street front.[15] The bay had an English vernacular air and disturbed the quiet, late-Georgian dignity of the front; Mackintosh did not share the growing admiration of English architects for the orderliness and ordinariness of late-Georgian terraced houses.

3. 78 Derngate: ground floor plans before and after alteration. Based on *The Ideal Home,* August 1920.

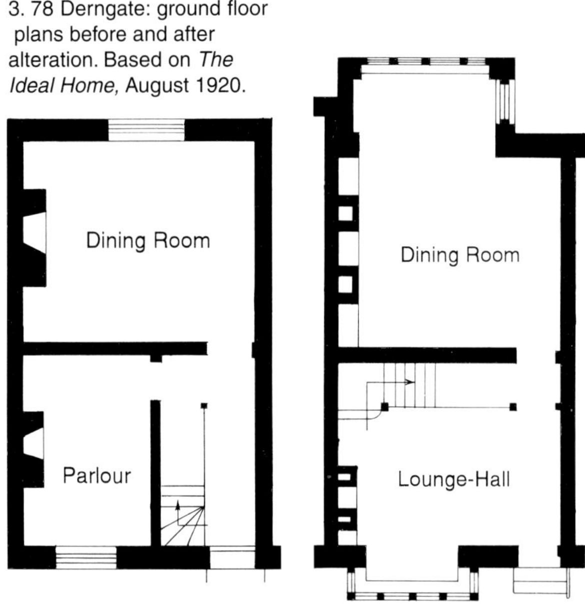

At the back the ground fell away, leaving the house four storeys high, and here Mackintosh added a three-storey bay with a balcony above (ill. 4). This provided a bigger kitchen and dining room; a deep covered balcony to the principal bedroom on the first floor; and an open balcony to the guest bedroom above. The back of the house faced south over parkland and the River Nene, and the view was almost sylvan; the covered balcony, Bassett-Lowke later wrote, "offers a most desirable venue for light breakfasts and suppers in the summer time."[16] The bay was covered with a smooth render; and the openings were simple rectangles without any mouldings. It was only a small piece of work, but it was white, rectilinear and designed for fresh air and the sun, and thus closer in style to the earliest white, rectilinear buildings of European Modernism than any other British building of its date.[17]

4. 78 Derngate: rear elevation after alteration (cat. 12b)

Put like this, the story is simple, and the bay at the back fits the picture of Mackintosh as a pioneer of the Modern Movement perfectly. But was it Mackintosh who was the pioneer? Bassett-Lowke was a committed Modernist, well-travelled in Europe, with a taste for quiet rationality and a definite idea of what he wanted. Inside 78 Derngate one can feel two minds at work: Mackintosh in the lounge-hall and the 1919 recasting of the guest bedroom with their colour, pattern and controlled intensity; Bassett-Lowke in the rest of the house with its quiet good sense, quality of materials and modern technology, none of which had ever interested Mackintosh. The bay at the back feels more like Bassett-Lowke than Mackintosh. An article on the house which reflects Bassett-Lowke's views specifically urged the superiority of a deep, covered balcony over the usual British type, "wooden or metal structures attached to the surface of the house, too small except to stand upon, and affording no protection from sun, wind or rain."[18] Mackintosh's balconies before and after Derngate were just such shallow, open structures.

78 Derngate was completed by March 1917; after that Mackintosh had no more architectural work during the war. To earn money, he and Margaret had begun producing designs for printed textiles whose vibrant colours owe a debt to Bakst and the Ballets Russes, their sometimes bold simplicity of form to Roger Fry's Omega Workshops.[19] And by 1916 he had started a series of watercolour paintings of flowers in still-life, whose strong and exuberant colours are Post-Impressionist or even Fauve in feeling, though they are also studio-based and precisely draughted.[20] The watercolours and the textile designs seem to reflect a shift, in these uncertain times, in Mackintosh's sense of himself, as if, in contact with avant-garde art and lacking other work, he was beginning to think of himself as an artist rather than an architect.

When peace came, however, Mackintosh tried to re-establish his architectural practice. In August 1919 he wrote that he had a lot of schemes in hand, but they were waiting until prices became more reasonable; the only architectural work for that year was an extension to a small house at East Grinstead for his friend the photographer, E.O. Hoppé.[21] Then, in January and February 1920, he was commissioned to design three separate studios or studio-houses next door to each other in Glebe Place. This was followed in March by a block of studios and studio-flats; and in June by a theatre. All of these, with the possible exception of the theatre, were to be built on a plot of land bounded on the north side by Glebe Place, on the east by Oakley Street and on the south by Upper Cheyne Row (ill. 5). The ground landlord was the Glebe of Chelsea.[22] This plot had been occupied, since the 18th century, by Cheyne House and its garden; in the late 19th century it was acquired by an eccentric architect and scientist, Dr John Samuel Phené, who built the so-called Mystery House on the corner of

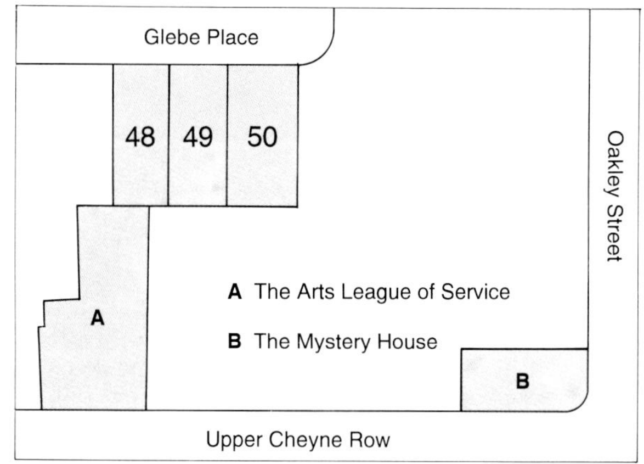

5. Site plan of Glebe Place showing Mackintosh's building plots. Based on Phené sale particulars of 1914.

Oakley Street and Upper Cheyne Row which he presented, implausibly, as the reconstruction of a Loire château once owned by his family (ill. 6).[23] Phené died in 1912, and in July 1914 the property was advertised for sale in 17 lots.[24] I do not know whether the property sold at that inauspicious time; but part or all of it must have come on the market again towards the end of 1919, leading to Mackintosh's commissions. By the middle of 1920, he had work in prospect to rival his busiest days with Honeyman and Keppie.

6. The Mystery House pre-1914

The story of these commissions has never been properly told. Writers on Mackintosh usually take the three drawings now in The British Museum as a convenient summary of Mackintosh's proposals; these are one drawing called *Block of Studios* (ill. 10) and two called *Three Chelsea Studios* (ills. 7 and 8).[25] But the story is almost certainly more complicated. The Hunterian Art Gallery has more than 80 working drawings for Mackintosh's buildings in Chelsea; it also has Mackintosh's office diary for 1920. Few of the drawings are dated, but these two sources between them provide the basis for a tentative chronology. And such a chronology raises the suspicion that the drawings for *Three Chelsea Studios* are misleading, for the elevations in those drawings labelled for Wood and Squire probably date from January or February 1920, and certainly no later than 12 June, while the elevations for the Arts League of Service probably date from December 1920 or later, and certainly no earlier than the middle of June. Thus, it is likely that they are not contemporaneous designs and that Mackintosh never envisaged that this ensemble could be built. It is simplest to tell the story of each commission in turn.

In January the painter Harold Squire asked Mackintosh to design a studio-house at what is now no. 49 Glebe Place.[26] The design seems to have gone through three stages. The first, which probably belongs to January and February, was for an expensive studio-house on two and three storeys with elevations like those in *Three Chelsea Studios*: a small gabled building in front of a larger, flat-fronted block with the studio occupying the first and second floors (ills. 7

and 8). (Since the buildings for Squire, Blunt and Wood were on the south side of Glebe Place, any studio windows providing north light would have to be in the street front.) The second scheme, which ran from March to the middle of June and is more fully developed in the surviving drawings, moved the studio-block forward to the street and put the domestic offices on the ground floor; the street front was not greatly altered and the big studio window was framed by a stepped brick architrave which hovers somewhere between Vienna, Holland and the later stages of the English Arts and Crafts movement (ill. 9).[27]

It appears that Squire's sister, a Mrs Evelyn Claude, was paying for the house, and that her purse was not as long as Squire or Mackintosh supposed. On 12 June Squire asked Mackintosh to redesign the scheme with a single-storey studio.[28] At this, the third stage, Mackintosh's nerve, or possibly his patience, failed. He set the studio back again from the street, giving it the form of a big shed with its north window reaching down to the ground, and put in front of it a strangely blank single-storey building containing a sitting-room and kitchen. This design, with the addition of two bedrooms perched on the flat roof, was built, and probably completed early in 1921.[29]

In February Mackintosh was asked to design a studio-house immediately west of Squire's plot, at what is now no. 48 Glebe Place. This was for another artist, Arthur Cadogan Blunt, who apparently specialised in the design of glass chandeliers, mirrors and the like.[30] It seems that Blunt did not need a north light and Mackintosh designed a three-storeyed, sash-windowed, rather Georgian-looking front for him which echoed the many modest 18th-century houses in Chelsea; he put the studio on the garden side and lit it with sash windows of quite unGeorgian proportions (ill. 9). However, in May, Blunt made a request typical of the 1920s: would Mackintosh incorporate some timbers from an old barn in the building? Mackintosh did so and consulted the District Surveyor and the London County Council; but at this point the job seems to have gone dead; after the end of May, his diary has nothing more to say about Blunt.[31]

Also in February, Mackintosh was approached by the sculptor Francis Derwent Wood about the site on the other side of Squire's, now no. 50 Glebe Place.[32] Wood did not want a studio-house, though Mackintosh's design looked like one; there was a sculptor's studio and workshop on the ground floor, lit from the north by a big expanse of window; and the upper floors were

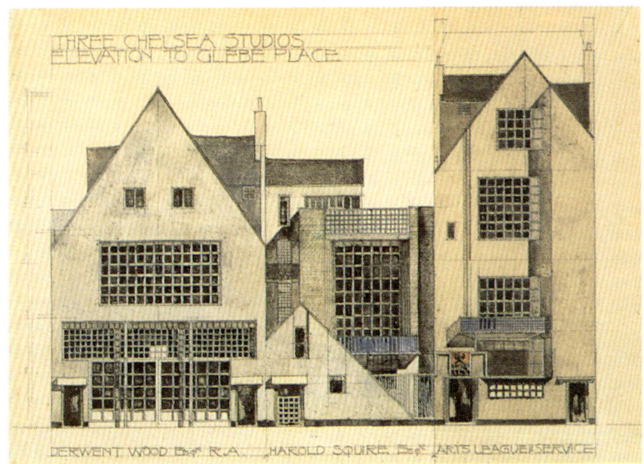

7. *Three Chelsea Studios*: elevation to Glebe Place (cat. 23)

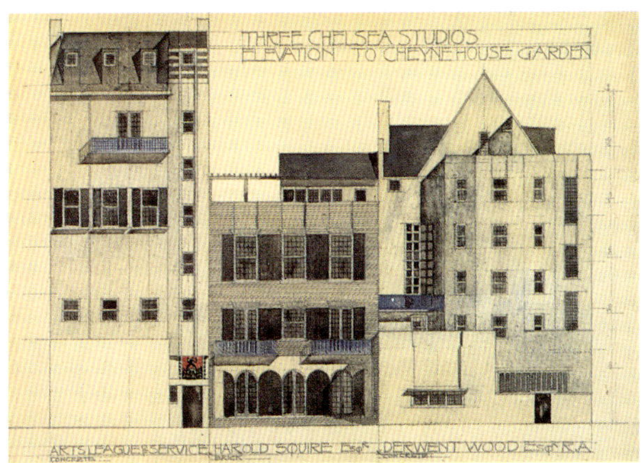

8. *Three Chelsea Studios*: elevation to Cheyne House Garden (cat. 24)

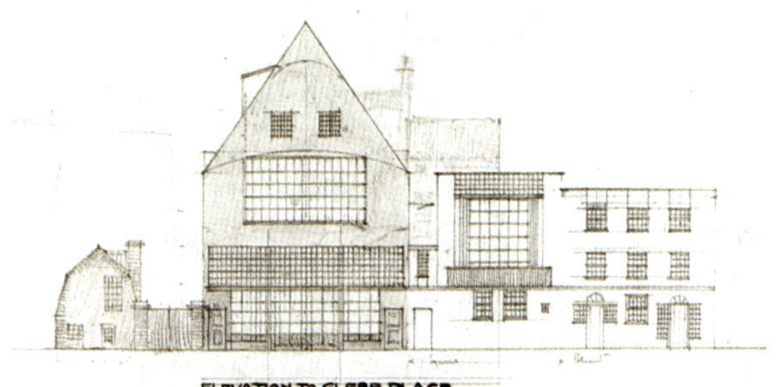

9. Studios of Francis Derwent Wood – detail of elevation of 48-50 Glebe Place (cat. 19)

given over to lettable painters' studios, with separate access. Mackintosh's first design was probably that shown in *Three Chelsea Studios* (ills. 7 and 8); in June Wood asked for something less and Mackintosh designed a new arrangement behind the same façade; on 17 June he showed the new plans to W.E. Clifton, Surveyor to the Glebe of Chelsea, who insisted on "more architectural qualities" in the elevation.[33] It was an understandable reaction. The glazing patterns were almost the only point of visual interest in Mackintosh's bare English vernacular design, as if he felt that the proportions and materials of these rectilinear grids, which fascinated him so, were enough. Mackintosh had used vernacular forms and glazing patterns in this way at The Hill House with the same result: homeliness and abstraction. There are drawings from late in 1920 which suggest that this design was on the verge of being built; but it was not, and Wood built a single-storey studio on the site a few years later.[34]

Mackintosh's next client was not an individual but a voluntary organisation, The Arts League of Service, which had been set up in 1919 "To Bring the Arts into Everyday Life".[35] The League organised exhibitions of young artists' work and ran a travelling theatre; its moving spirit was a

round, lively Chilean woman called Ana Berry; and the painters J.D. Fergusson and Randolph Schwabe and the musician Eugene Goossens, all friends of Mackintosh, were all involved. On 27 March Mackintosh showed Miss Berry, Fergusson and Margaret Morris over the bizarre Mystery House, which they were thinking of taking over, and he actually made sketch designs for them to do so.[36] But then, four days later, Ana Berry asked him to design a scheme at the west end of the property, on the site of the now-demolished Cheyne House. And this was the most exciting commission of all: a large block of studio-flats and studios, to be run as a co-operative.[37]

The site was narrow, and awkward for studios, facing east more than north, and the new building seems to have been restricted to the site of the old, perhaps by a building agreement.[38] During April and May, Mackintosh plied Anna Berry with drawings as the scheme developed into the settled form represented by the *Block of Studios* drawing, though that may be of a much later date (ill. 10). On the west side he piled four studio-flats on top of each other, with living accommodation on mezzanines; this gave the vertical strips of windows in Upper Cheyne Row. On the east side there were 19 studios looking out over the garden; and there were 27 studios in all.[39] The height of the building and the steep slope of the northern roof both corresponded to the maximum limits set out in the London Building Act of 1894;

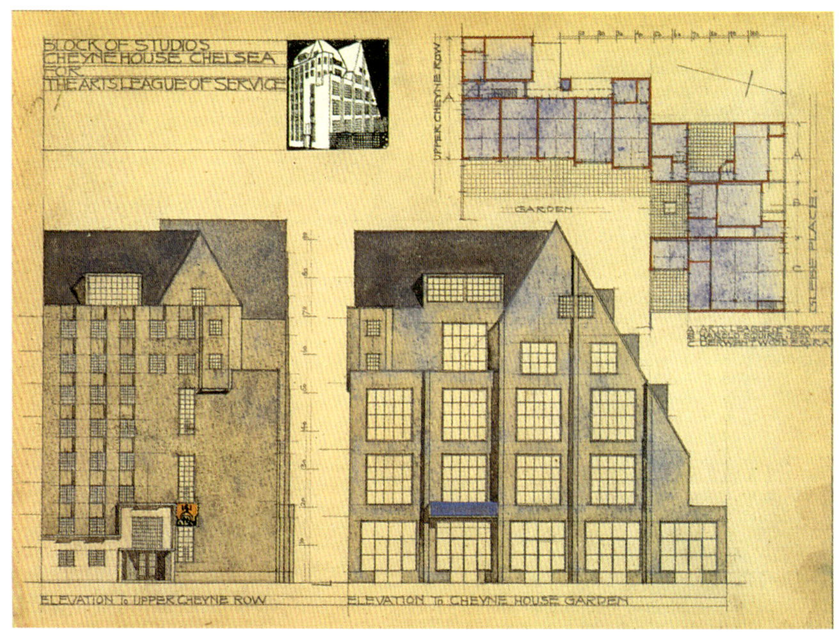

10. *Block of Studios* (cat. 20)

Mackintosh was crowding as much onto the site as possible.[40] But he had, coming from Scotland, a language for this sort of piling up: the high gable, the stepping back of the garden front and the chamfered, overhanging corner of the fourth floor evoke memories of 17th-century tenements in Edinburgh; while the arrangement of the two principal fronts, one all studio-windows, the other vertical window-strips, recalled the north and west fronts of his own Glasgow School of Art.

In June he went to see the Ministry of Housing, perhaps hoping for grant-aid; in September there were objections from the ground landlord that the building was unsuitable for the area; but these were later overcome. And by the end of the year it looked as if the building could go ahead if the money could be raised.[41] But no further progress is recorded.

The last Chelsea commission recorded in Mackintosh's diary came from Margaret Morris, partner of J.D. Fergusson and pioneer of avant-garde dance in Britain; it was for a small theatre to go on the Glebe of Chelsea's land, though it is not clear where (ill. 11).[42] At first glance, it seems quite different from anything Mackintosh had done before; but the stripped and monumental forms and the plan of the auditorium recall Mackintosh's 1898 competition designs for Glasgow's International Exhibition. The most obviously new, and problematic, element in the design is the splayed architrave, which relates uneasily to the pepperpot towers and makes no sense, or at least no good sense, as a screen to the two spiral staircases. Like so much else in 1920, the theatre went unbuilt.

There remains one scheme which was never clearly recorded in Mackintosh's diary and to which, therefore, a firm date cannot be given. We have met it already in the discussion of the *Three Chelsea Studios* drawings (ills. 7 and 8). There it was labelled for the Arts League of Service. There is no

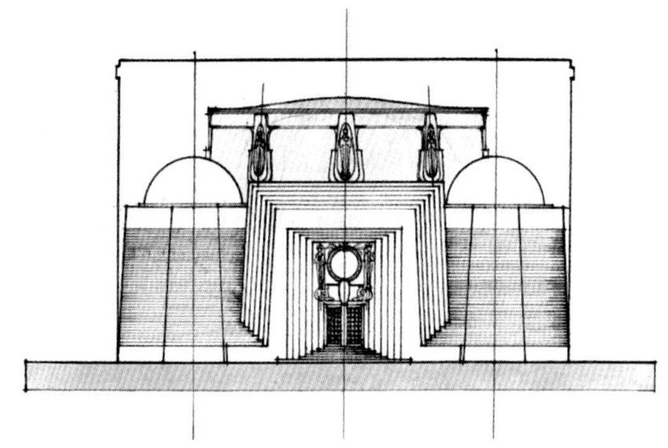

11. Theatre for Margaret Morris: detail of front elevation (cat. 27)

documentary evidence to tell us when the League commissioned this tower-like block or how its story fits into that of the earlier block. But we can establish a probable chronology. It cannot have been designed before June 1920, for it stands on the site which, until at least the end of May, was intended for the Blunt studio-house. It may have been designed in December 1920, for the Hunterian has two drawings which are variant designs for the Glebe Place front, suggesting that they belong to the early stages of the design. Now both drawings also show Harold Squire's studio-house at no. 49 in its final form. As this was only reached at the end of November 1920, the Arts League scheme probably dates from December 1920 or later.[43] It cannot be later than December 1922, when the *Three Chelsea Studios* drawings were included in an *Exhibition of Contemporary British Architecture* at the Royal Institute of British Architects.[44] Therefore it was probably designed sometime between December 1920 and December 1922.

Mackintosh's studio-houses were very different from others that were being built in Chelsea at this date. In The Vale, Mallord Street, and Mulberry Walk, north of the King's Road, there are groups of houses built just before and after the First World War, many of them for artists. They are in neat, silver-grey and red brick; the difficult and clever effects of Arts and Crafts architecture round 1900 have been set aside in favour of expertise and restfulness, the neo-Georgian and neo-Tudor tastes; each group reads as the work of a single hand, and they furnish coherent, almost cosy, street scenes.[45]

Mackintosh's designs, on the other hand, showed a deliberate variety, of materials, massing, scale and style, almost as if they were designed by different people. In this respect they were much closer to the work of an architect whom he must have known by reputation all his life, C.R. Ashbee. Between 1893 and 1913 Ashbee designed some 14 schemes for houses, studio-houses and flats on Cheyne Walk, and built seven of them. He thought in streetscape terms, creating a medley of buildings next door to each other, some in a bare Arts and Crafts style, others neo-Georgian, all various in form and mock-modest in detail; anyone who looked carefully would see a difference between inside and out, a playing with appearances, such as informed some of the best of Mackintosh's Glasgow buildings (ill. 12). Ashbee could create a strong but subtle sense of place; after nos. 71-5 Cheyne Walk were bombed in the Second

World War, a journalist lamented: "Those fronts, those oddly fascinating fronts which aped nothing Chelsea and yet seemed to breathe its atmosphere so intensely – gone!"[46] Mackintosh probably did not share Ashbee's peculiarly literary and historical sense of Chelsea, but the picturesque, country-town grouping of his designs is remarkably strong for someone who had not created streetscape before. Most evenings, on their way to eat at the Blue Cockatoo, Mackintosh and Margaret would walk past the other Ashbee group, nos 37-9 Cheyne Walk. It is hard to believe that Mackintosh did not learn from them.

12. C.R. Ashbee: 71-75 Cheyne Walk 1897-1913

The *Exhibition of Contemporary British Architecture* at the R.I.B.A. provides an appropriate ending to this story. The exhibition was announced in September 1922; some weeks later, architects were asked to confine their exhibits if possible to photographs – an exhibition of contemporary American architecture at the R.I.B.A in 1921 had shown the power of photographs with the public.[47] Mackintosh could, presumably, have exhibited photographs of his Glasgow work, or even of his unsatisfactory studio-house for Squire; but he chose to send *Three Chelsea Studios* and *Block of Studios* framed as a single exhibit. As it turned out the exhibition was largely a display of pre-war work by leading Edwardians, including Newton, Lutyens, Mewes and Davis, Sir Edwin Cooper, Clough Williams-Ellis. One can imagine Mackintosh at the exhibition, alienated and dismayed. Here were the achievements of British architecture in the first decade of the 20th century when the Free

Style which he loved was a waning force and Vienna was his guiding star; here it was in photographs, substantial civic and monumental work, real and convincing, the grey stone expertly cut. All he had to show was four unexecuted buildings brought together in drawings which, however fetching, could never have been realised. Reviewing the exhibition, H.S. Goodhart-Rendel wrote: "Two exhibits sent by Mr C.R. Mackintosh looked curiously old-fashioned, and recalled to mind the illustrations which one finds in turning over the pages of the early volumes of "The Studio"."[48] He might have written that the other exhibits recalled the early volumes of *Country Life* and *Architectural Review*, the arbiters of Edwardian architectural taste in whose pages Mackintosh's work had never appeared.

And yet I do not believe that Mackintosh had entirely lost his way. Rather, when he turned back to Ashbee and c. 1900 for help, he was on the point of finding it again. He lost his way in Glasgow, in those last years when he could not handle work in the office of Honeyman, Keppie and Mackintosh. The Chelsea years witnessed a slow, moving and, in the end, unfinished process of recovery. With the Geddes designs he had no brief, and was under considerable personal stress; Philip Mairet, who was working in the same room as Mackintosh in the summer of 1915, remembered the smell of drink on his breath.[49] At 78 Derngate he was working with a man of definite views and oddly different tastes, and the outside of the house was perhaps not clearly his; inside, the two rooms where he was given his head showed that his decorative ability was not diminished. But in Chelsea he was working for artists and friends, building studio-houses which combined two of the most inspirational themes in his work, art and domesticity.[50] He had lived there for five years; here was something to build on. Ashbee's houses seemed to demonstrate a point from which, a place in which, he could develop a new career. If he had stayed for longer, and found the right clients, he might have found his way as a studio-architect in Chelsea, and London would have had a building worthy of him.

In the end something else happened. In 1923 the Mackintoshes went on an extended holiday to the South of France and decided to stay on. Mackintosh's last works, strong in character and worked at with great intensity, were watercolours of the Mediterranean landscape.

Alan Crawford

Footnotes

(HAG: Coll. Hunterian Art Gallery)

1. Robert Macleod, *Charles Rennie Mackintosh* (Feltham, Middlesex 1968), p. 150.

2. Thomas Howarth, *Charles Rennie Mackintosh and the Modern Movement* (second edition, London 1977), pp. 193-6; Alistair Moffat, *Remembering Charles Rennie Mackintosh: An Illustrated Biography* (Lanark 1989), pp. 80-81, 83 and 93 gives additional information about Mackintosh and drink.

3. "Embittered": Howarth, *Mackintosh*, p. 193; "passed by": Gavin Stamp, 'Mackintosh, Burnet and Modernity' in John Lowrey (ed.), *Architectural Heritage III: The Age of Mackintosh* (Edinburgh 1992), pp. 20-24.

4. Margaret Macdonald Mackintosh to Anna Geddes, 14 January 1915. Geddes Papers, National Library of Scotland, MS 10582.

5. As note 4.

6. Mackintosh to William Davidson, 21 July 1915, HAG; Home Office register of correspondence for 1915 (HO 46/186 Aliens Restriction), entries for 24 June, 9 July, 6 and 9 October 1915, Public Record Office, Kew.

7. Letter of 21 July 1915, HAG.

8. Designs for Geddes: Philip Mairet to Murray Grigor, 2 March 1967 published in Moffat, *Mackintosh*, pp. 93-4; Mackintosh and India: Mackintosh to William Davidson, 5 August 1915, HAG. The arguments for connecting the two *Arcaded Street* designs with Geddes are set out in Pamela Robertson, 'The Unknown Mackintosh' *Christie's International Magazine* 1991, vol. 8, pp. 8-9.

9. The gates at Sanchi would have been known to Mackintosh from the illustration in W.R. Lethaby's *Architecture, Mysticism and Myth* (London 1891).

10. The frames also recall Viennese striped borders such as Hoffmann's exhibition designs in *Dekorative Kunst* 1899, vol. 4, p. 38, and his carpets in the villa for Hugo Henneberg illustrated in Eduard Sekler, *Josef Hoffmann: The Architectural Work* (Princeton, N. J. 1985), ill. 48. These striped borders are also an obvious exemplar for the 1919 guest bedroom at 78 Derngate, Northampton.

11. Mackintosh's studio was 2 Hans Studios, 43A Glebe Place, and was probably built in the 1890s by the Arts and Crafts sculptor and potter Conrad Dressler (English Heritage London Division, Historian's file: Kensington and Chelsea: 70). Margaret Mackintosh's studio was 2 Cedar Studios, 45 Glebe Place.

12. Howarth, *Mackintosh*, p. 198 says that "there is no evidence to support the popular assumption that they were in difficult financial circumstances"; but letters from Mackintosh to William Davidson of 19 June 1915, 1 April 1919 and 12 August 1919, HAG, show that he needed, at times, to borrow money urgently.

13. Howarth, *Mackintosh*, pp. 199 and 215; Roger Billcliffe, *Mackintosh Textile Designs* (San Francisco 1993), p. 12 identifies the young architect as Allan Ure.

14. For Bassett-Lowke, architecture and design, see Louise Campbell, 'A Model Patron: Bassett-Lowke, Mackintosh and Behrens' *Journal of the Decorative Arts Society* 1986, vol. 10, pp. 1-9.

15. Plans in *The Ideal Home* August 1920, p. 54.

16. Typescript of 22 August 1939, HAG.

17. The fullest account of the work done for Bassett-Lowke is two articles each entitled 'Now and Then: A Transformation' in *The Ideal Home* for August and September 1920.

18. *The Ideal Home*, September 1920, p. 93. Much of the text of this article is identical with Bassett-Lowke's typescript of 22 August 1939 at HAG.

19. Roger Billcliffe, *Mackintosh Textile Designs* (San Francisco 1993).

20. Roger Billcliffe, *Mackintosh Watercolours* (London 1979).

21. Mackintosh to Davidson, 15 August 1919, HAG; the extension for Hoppé was at Little Hedgecourt, East Grinstead, East Sussex, see Roderick Gradidge, 'The last of Mackintosh' *The Field*, 8 December 1984, pp. 11-13.

22. That is, it was church property. For the extent of the Glebe's property, see the Ground Plan of London, Greater London Record Office.

23. Thea Holme, *Chelsea* (London 1972), pp. 241-2.

24. Tyler & Co. Sale particulars for "Old Cheyne House, The Mystery House and King Henry VIII's Hunting Lodge also valuable building sites", 8 July 1914, Chelsea Public Library.

25. See Howarth, *Mackintosh*, p. 212, where it is said that the *Three Chelsea Studios* drawings "give a clear indication of his intentions"; Macleod, *Mackintosh*, p. 148; and Jackie Cooper, *Mackintosh Architecture: The Complete Buildings and Selected Projects* (London 1978), pp. 104-5.

26. Diary, 8 January 1920, HAG.

27. The first scheme is represented in the Hunterian by L(e)4; the second by L(e)13, 14, 22 and 23 among many others. My dating of the two schemes is based on the fact that during March Mackintosh had tracings and linen prints made of his plans and sent them to the district surveyor, quantity surveyor and specialist suppliers. The Hunterian drawings show the second scheme developed in sufficient detail for this, but not the first. For a Viennese stepped architrave which Mackintosh would probably have known, see the reception room designed by Josef Hoffmann in Charles Holme (ed.), *The Art-Revival in Austria* (London 1906), C18.

28. Diary, HAG.

29. HAG, L(e)5 and 24 represent the final stages of the design. Harold Squire first appears in the Voter's Register for this property in the autumn of 1921. The building survives, but the front building was raised to two storeys in 1924 and the studio building has been altered internally.

30. Howarth, *Mackintosh*, p. 207.

31. Diary, 14, 19, 22 and 31 May 1920, HAG.

32. Diary, 24 February 1920, HAG. Francis Derwent Wood (1871-1926) may have known Mackintosh from the late 1890s, when he taught modelling at Glasgow School of Art; he was Professor of Sculpture at the Royal College of Art from 1918 to 1923.

33. Diary, 15 and 17 June 1920, HAG. Drawings for Wood after this date show a more compact scheme than *Three Chelsea Studios*. In and for some time after 1920, Wood lived at 18 Carlyle Square and had a studio at 27 Glebe Place.

34. See photograph no. 74/2541, Greater London Record Office. The present no. 50 Glebe Place, which dates from 1985-7, incorporates rainwater-heads with the initials "DW" and the date 1923.

35. Arts League of Service, *Design and Art* (London 1928), and especially pp. 46-55.

36. Diary, 27 March and 25 May 1920, HAG. A sketchbook by Mackintosh at HAG includes survey sketches of the Mystery House made on 18 February 1920, (HAG A6, pp. 64-66).

37. Howarth, *Mackintosh*, pp. 210-13; Arts League of Service, *Design and Art* (London 1928) pp. 64-6.

38. "The site could be bought fairly cheaply; but there was a clause in the agreement which allowed for only a very small section to be built on." Arts League of Service, *Design and Art*, p. 51; Mackintosh's block covered almost exactly the former site of Old Cheyne House, as if it was restricted to it. Some years later, the garden site was built over with houses in a neo-Tudor manner, nos 2-14 Upper Cheyne Row.

39. This account of the accommodation is based on plans at HAG: L(c)7, 26, 27, 28 and 29; they vary in some details from the plan and elevations in the *Block of Studios* drawing.

40. Clause 41 of the Act specified a diagonal line running from the back of the site at an angle of 63½°, and clause 47 a height of 80 feet excluding two storeys in the roof and any ornamental towers, turrets and other architectural features. See Roger Harper, *Victorian Building Regulations* (London 1985), Table 14.

41. Diary, 1 June, 1 September and 20 December 1920, HAG.

42. Diary, 2 and 5 June 1920, HAG.

43. HAG, L(c)35 and 39; a rear elevation of the block, formerly in the collection of Thomas Howarth, shows the same arrangement, see Christie's, *The Dr Thomas Howarth Collection* (catalogue of a sale, London, 17 February 1994), lot no. 79.

44. *Three Chelsea Studios* and *Block of Studios* were framed together, and part of a label from the frame survives in Mackintosh's hand referring to the exhibition. According to *Architectural Review* 1923, vol. 53, p. 31, Mackintosh sent two exhibits, but the identity of the second is not known.

45. The architects principally involved in these streets were Alfred Cox and F.E. Williams; see Bridget Cherry and Nikolaus Pevsner, *The Buildings of England: London: 3: North West* (London 1991), p. 586.

46. *Illustrated Carpenter and Builder*, 23 May 1941. For Ashbee's Cheyne Walk houses generally, see Alan Crawford, *C.R. Ashbee: Architect, Designer and Romantic Socialist* (New Haven and London 1985), pp. 237-59.

47. *Architects' Journal* 20 September 1922, p. 386 and *Builder* 8 December 1922, p. 863.

48. *Architectural Review* 1923, vol. 53, p. 31.

49. Moffat, *Remembering Charles Rennie Mackintosh*, p. 93.

50. These themes had been developed in the interiors of 120 Mains Street, the House for an Art Lover, 6 Florentine Terrace and the Ingram Street and Willow Tea Rooms; also Mackintosh had produced speculative sketch designs for two studio-houses, published in *Dekorative Kunst* 1902, vol. 9, pp. 211-13.

'UNCLE WHYNNE'

A MEMOIR OF W.J. BASSETT-LOWKE

1. W.J. Bassett-Lowke with his nieces Vivian (left) and Janet 1925

by JANET BASSETT-LOWKE

My uncle, Wenman Joseph Bassett-Lowke (1877-1953), was trained as an engineer and built up a successful business in Northampton producing scale models of all kinds during the first half of this century. In 1915 he commissioned Charles Rennie Mackintosh to redesign completely a small terraced house in Northampton, no. 78 Derngate.

Later he wished to build a larger house in the modern style. I was told that his first thought again was for Mackintosh, who was not then available, and that he had to search elsewhere, eventually discovering the German architect, Dr Peter Behrens, who planned his second marital home, New Ways, in Wellingborough Road, Northampton. Uncle did take from Derngate some of the work of Mackintosh.

Sadly he had no children, and my sisters and I were his three nieces, daughters of his younger brother, Harold.

2. 78 Derngate: lounge-hall 1917

A Memoir of W.J. Bassett-Lowke

3. 78 Derngate: section of design for lounge-hall stencil (cat. 40)

In the spring of 1917, when my uncle was 39, he married and went to live at 78 Derngate, Northampton. His bride was Florence Jane Jones, whose father, Charles Jones, was founder of the well-known English shoemakers, Crockett and Jones. We children were very young when uncle and aunt resided at the Mackintosh house, but I was told by my mother that we were taken round as toddlers, even into the famous guest room with the stripes overhead! However my first and clearest memory of no. 78 was that it was quite different from other houses. There was the enormous light-fitting which filled the ceiling of the lounge-hall, and drew immediate attention as you walked in. Then I used to count the squares of the hall screen, with its sparkling glass pattern, which masked the stairs going up to the next floor. It was an adventure to go up those stairs and into the bathroom on the first floor, so clean and bright with its pristine whiteness, and peep through the holes in the screen as you came down again (ill. 2). I looked forward to visits to no. 78 as our aunt made delicious teas. Then afterwards, if we had behaved well, uncle would bring out some of his fascinating mechanical toys, which jumped about and played tricks as he wound them up. But so soon it would be time to put them away in their neat boxes and for us to go home.

One of the rooms in our home in a street nearby was not unlike the dining room at no. 78. It was on the first floor and was planned by our parents to be the 'parlour'. Our father and mother had been engaged for about two years without progress when uncle laid a wager with father that he would never marry mother. The amount for those days was not small – £100. Early in the 1900s it was quite usual to have a long engagement, and in the fourth year, 1913, when the great day was finally arranged, uncle graciously accepted he had lost and told our parents that he planned to spend the money furnishing a room for them as a wedding present.

So the first floor room was restyled. The walls were covered with a greenish paper with discreet stripes, the paintwork was skilfully changed to represent light oak, in harmony with the furniture arriving from Germany. Each piece was constructed on straight lines without any curves, eminently practical and beautifully made. The top of the tall sideboard had a broad, two-door shelved display section. Its doors each had five vertical panels of thick bevelled glass. Below, on either side, was a tall cupboard and in the centre an open shelved area with three long drawers beneath. The locks were of brass, marked Dittmar Mobel Fabr. The fitted sofa unit had a display area above, with a small cupboard at each end with bevelled glass panels. Pressed into this unit was the typical German square-shape sofa, covered in green cord velvet, as were the seats of the two carving chairs and two dining chairs. The oblong grandfather clock, which had a deep booming sound striking both hours and half hours, completed the suite. Each item of furniture, made in solid oak, had a pattern of inlaid black bands along the top and the sideboard doors were quartered with a central oval inlay. Even after 80 years of usage all adjustable shelves still fit perfectly and the doors open and close as easily as if they had been made yesterday.

Thinking back to the past about this room – 'the German room' was always its designation – how well it had been planned, the fine quality of the pieces, all in place and in use before the First World War, I tend to believe that my uncle's maxim of 'Fitness for Purpose' was a strong focus early in his life, and that this could well have been the ideal which drew him towards the work of Charles Rennie Mackintosh.

What did surprise me about uncle, who was often referred to as the 'King of Lilliput' and who

had this famous shop in London, a mecca for boys of all ages, was that he really did not understand children. He had one or two stock remarks which he used to bring out for us, his young relatives, from whom he would always expect the same pat answers. When he wanted a photograph of children with toys or models he would often come to father, who was an excellent photographer. Sometimes we would be the subjects, mostly my youngest sister June, who was several years my junior. Directly W.J. had stage-managed the pictures he would hardly stay a minute. With a quick word to my father or mother, he would hurry away down the path, coat-tails flying.

4. Advertising label for W.J. Bassett-Lowke Ltd (cat. 33.c)

Later, as we began to grow up and do things, uncle showed more interest in us. We all liked school and, under father's coaching, became promising at tennis and particularly talented at swimming. At the time when uncle was chairman of the Baths Committee of Northampton Borough Council, sister Vivian was becoming the real star at swimming. She worked her way up from local championships to Midland District competitions and beyond to become a National champion. This naturally pleased uncle, and the year I was leaving school he decided to take Vivian and me on a short cruise to the fjords of Norway. Vivian gained this treat because of her swimming successes. My task was to write an essay for uncle, "Impressions of My First Cruise". It was the first time I had had the chance to talk to him at any length and he asked me what I intended to do. During our chat I mentioned my disappointment at not being able to go to university. I did not think he had taken much notice. However, on the last day of the trip, which had been exciting for Vivian and myself, he said he had been thinking about my future and would I like to come and work for him?

So that is how I started at Bassett-Lowke Ltd, working, mornings only, at the Northampton headquarters for a modest half a guinea a week. I had a small desk in the book-keeper's office and helped him. After I had been working there a few weeks, uncle popped his head round the door and called me into his private office. He had read my screed about the Norwegian cruise and suggested I should take a course on journalism and writing. He went on to suggest a postal course and handed me an advertisement clipping about a writing institute. So I took his advice.

5. *Nipper:* the first Bassett-Lowke passenger-carrying railway *c.* 1905

Another day he said to me: "Come up to New Ways. Your auntie has a bicycle she won't use any more and you can have it." It was smart and royal blue, but a little small for me as aunt was only about five feet tall! Little did I think at the time that there might be something behind this gift, but before long uncle was requiring me to cycle down to meet him at the railway station at around 8.20 a.m. with my notebook. I had to take down any letters he required and receive a list of other instructions for the day. There he would be, the smart businessman, standing impatiently at the door of his train compartment with the usual wad of papers. Ten minutes for the letters, the relevant notes thrust into my hand, then the final quick-fire instructions and he would be away, waving from the open carriage window as the 8.45 a.m. for Euston steamed out of the station.

All the while I was gradually learning about him. He had left school quite early, at 13, and joined the family engineering and boiler-making business in Kingswell Street, Northampton, as an apprentice. He told me that he had enjoyed school. One of his teachers in particular had encouraged him to read and to realise the

value of books. When he had been at work for a short time, his father let him make a change and go into a local architect's office. He was 17 then and spent 18 months there before deciding to return to engineering. From boyhood, he had been keen on model-making and, while serving his apprenticeship, he developed a little business selling small castings and miniature boiler fittings for model engines and pumps. Harry Franklin, his father's young book-keeper, joined him in this project and they were allowed to display these items in the firm's shop window. Later, when he went to Crompton & Co. of Chelmsford, to gain further experience in electrical engineering with the outdoor staff at York and Leeds, Franklin kept the embryo business going.

W.J.'s mother, a former private governess, had been abroad before her marriage and it was perhaps from her that he inherited his love of foreign countries. Certainly he travelled extensively in Europe. When he was only 23 he went to the famous Paris Exhibition of 1900 and there met manufacturers of toys and models willing to do business with him. The year before he had encountered Percival Marshall, just starting up as the editor and proprietor of a new magazine, *The Model Engineer*. Here was the means of advertising his wares more widely. Also in the company of Percival Marshall, he met with Henry Greenly and engaged him as consulting engineer.

Together with other interested parties, they sought to promote outdoor garden railways (ill. 5). This was before the Great War and some of the railways they helped to pioneer, notably the Ravenglass and Eskdale in the Lake District and the Romney, Hythe and Dymchurch (Henry Greenly's triumph), we still know today.

Help in the first stages of W.J.'s business came from his father, for many of the castings he needed were produced from the J.T. Lowke foundry in Kingswell Street. In 1909 the Bassett-Lowke firm was set up, with Mr J.G. Sears of the True Form Boot Co. as first chairman. So, at the outbreak of war in 1914, the works and office in Northampton were in being and also, through the assistance of Mr Sears, the famous 'London Branch' in High Holborn had become a reality. From 1914 to 1918 there was war work and the firm's capability in engineering was used in the production of precision instruments. For some time there had been in my uncle's fertile mind the plans for Bassett-Lowke to develop exact-scale model masterpieces for exhibitions, museums and businesses, a field in which they became pre-eminent. This was in addition to the model railways, engines and ships, which filled many leisure hours for schoolboys and fathers alike.

This was the firm I was drawn into during the 1930s – varied and often fascinating, even to a girl. I was lucky to have opportunities to watch model work in all its stages – the delicate building of a ship from the rough wood of the hull to the finished shining model, with all its tiny fittings, ready to be displayed in the window of the headquarters of some great shipping company in London or elsewhere. B.L.'s tackled every kind of model – a working coal mine, the city of Coventry in miniature, a railway with a train in silver to run round the dining table of an Indian maharajah – these are just three examples of the variety. There was plenty to write about! After my 'apprenticeship', going through the different office departments, I was moved to assist uncle's secretary. Those were the days of helping with advertisements, articles, books and lectures and I often typed his personal letters on a vivid yellow notepaper with his New Ways heading in black plus a bright red spot!

Horoscopes interested W.J. He also placed reliance on graphology. Every so often he would send specimens of the handwriting of his friends, and also members of the staff, to the Institute of Graphology in London to be analysed. He was to a certain extent colour blind, but I believe he could see the startling yellow of his notepaper.

Recently, I was looking through some of my uncle's Christmas cards. These were his feature every year, and those on his very long Christmas list always looked

6. Greetings card (cat. 31.b)

forward to this annual 'offering' with eager anticipation. My favourite of them all was the one designed for 1922 by Charles Rennie Mackintosh (ill. 6), and second on my list was that by Ernest Noble in blue and black. This showed an extremely good caricature of uncle holding his beloved cine-camera which travelled everywhere with him. The colour most used among those I was studying was yellow, and several showed sketches of his business and his home, and photos of his regular cruises in far-off places. I remember him so well as he was in those days – agile and quick-thinking, a charming man, not always kindly, but endowed with a puckish smile and good manners. He was tall, slim and of athletic build, but not a sportsman. Though an ardent traveller and a very good walker, he never owned a car, nor learned to drive, preferring to go by train or bus, or failing that by taxi.

As my regard for the company grew, W.J. encouraged me, and we became good companions. I can remember on Monday evenings we used to – in his words – "drop by" to have a look at the Repertory Theatre's first performance of the week. We would pop into Box 'A' and watch the first act. Then he would say he must be off to get home on time for supper, but said I could stay on if I liked, and quite often I did.

WJ. was one of Northampton's businessmen who became enthusiastic about the work and achievements of the Rotary movement and he became a Founder Member in the early 1920s of the town's first Rotary club. He was interested in Rotary International and attended conferences on the continent and later went to the U.S.A. to a major gathering in Minneapolis. He was among several Rotarians who decided to attempt, with the help of other Northamptonians, to establish repertory players at the Royal Theatre and Opera House, and this small Victorian theatre became in 1927 the place where repertory was started, and still flourishes. W.J. was at the inaugural meeting and became a Founder Director on the first Board.

7. G.B. Shaw and Mrs Bassett-Lowke outside 78 Derngate 1922

8. 78 Derngate: guest bedroom furniture displayed in the Hunterian Art Gallery

W.J. was said to be the most travelled man in the town, knowing Europe from the North Cape to Budapest, and, brought up in the radical tradition, he joined the Labour party by way of the Fabian Society, becoming a member in 1910. He met George Bernard Shaw and, of the interesting people who visited him in the early 1920s at Derngate, perhaps the most famous was G.B.S. who stayed the weekend when addressing a meeting in 1923. When a dashing young reporter asked the great man how he had slept in Mackintosh's striped guest bedroom (ill. 8), G.B.S. is reputed to have answered "with my eyes shut!". Uncle kept in touch with him and went down to Ayot St Lawrence to visit and whenever Shaw came to Northampton, he was the guest of uncle and aunt. W.J. wrote to him at the time of his 86th birthday, sending an invitation to attend the Socialist summer school, and received a typically Shavian postcard in reply: "Dear Bassett-Lowke, I am too dammed old to go summer schooling nowadays, and I can hardly believe you are an elderly gentleman of 64. However, it is pleasant to hear that you and your consort are still going strong. I forget everything now in 10 minutes, but not the happy days in Northampton. Dotty and doddering but still able to write a bit. G. Bernard Shaw." There is a list of credits after W.J.'s name too long to mention in full. "M.I. Loco E." followed his name as a matter of course, also Founder Member of the Design and Industries Association and then the honour of Fellow of the Royal Society of Arts. Also, for several years, W.J. did much useful work as Councillor for the Borough of Northampton. In 1930, at the age of 53, he decided to fight St Lawrence's Ward for the Socialists and was elected. Two years later the wards were rearranged and he then stood for the St George's Ward. As chairman of the Baths Committee he was involved in work which interested him greatly, for three new buildings were to go up on the Upper Mounts: the Public Baths, Fire Station and Police Station.

9. Northampton Municipal Baths

A nationwide competition for architects was held and won by Messrs J.C. Prestwich of Leigh, who designed the new baths in a style after the chairman's own heart (ill. 9). It was a task too which fired his tenacity, to make sure the building was finished according to his own standards. Nearly 70 years on, the building still deserves the title which clings, the 'New Baths'. W.J. Bassett-Lowke became an alderman and in due course, in 1948, was offered the mayoralty of the Borough. He was pleased to have been asked, but, because of the health of his wife, declined.

As for his second marital home, New Ways, Sir Hugh Casson visited this "first modern house to be built in England" in the early 1950s when the house was 25 years old and uncle getting on in years. I agree with Sir Hugh's view that uncle and aunt had built a house that was well designed and comfortable. W.J. first had Mackintosh in mind as architect but by the mid 1920s Mackintosh was abroad, and so uncle set about the task of finding another such architect, without success in this country. It was in a German magazine, the 1913 *Yearbook* of the Deutscher Werkbund, that he found examples of the work of the architect Professor Dr Peter Behrens and

10. New Ways: garden elevation 1926

determined to meet him. With his Northampton builder Henry Green, W.J. proceeded to the continent in 1924 and met Behrens who was pleased to undertake the commission. The architect did not come to England but drew up the plans quickly and almost immediately this pioneer house began to take shape. Uncle had an excellent though worried builder, who was reluctant to be doing work against his rather conservative nature. But his client was adamant and New Ways was built exactly as planned, and today the present satisfied young owners pay tribute to the excellence of the materials and the building, which also met the high standards of its designer. During both uncle and aunt's lifetimes, I visited the house on many occasions and often stayed for a few days at a time. I remember it as a draught-free, easy, bright spacious home, the embodiment of W.J.'s maxim through life of 'Fitness for Purpose', with a certain modern beauty about the interiors. New Ways is still a very private home, though it is interesting to learn that there are plans afoot for no. 78 Derngate to be presented to the public in the not-too-distant future. I do not think that uncle would have been against this!

Janet Bassett-Lowke

The author is currently working on a memoir of Bassett-Lowke Ltd and would be pleased to hear from interested parties. Please write c/o Hunterian Art Gallery, University of Glasgow, Glasgow, G12 8QQ.

CATALOGUE

Design for a lampstandard *c.* 1915 (cat. 6.c)

Catalogue

All of the drawings exhibited are by C.R. Mackintosh with the exceptions of (8) and (32).

Unless otherwise credited all of the drawings form part of The Mackintosh Estate gifted to the University of Glasgow in 1947 by the Mackintoshes' nephew and residual legatee, Sylvan MacNair.

Dimensions are given in centimetres, height x width. Unless otherwise stated the support is cream paper.

1 ***The War: Its Social Tasks and Problems:***
Summer Meeting syllabus 1915
Lent by Strathclyde University Archives

2 **C.R. Mackintosh to William Davidson, Windyhill, Kilmacolm** August 1915
Signed and dated
Presented by Margaret and Winifred Davidson, 1990

3 ***A Warehouse Block in an Arcaded Street:***
front elevation *c.* 1915
Pencil, ink and watercolour; 26.0 x 70.5; Signed
Purchased with the support of the National Fund for Acquisitions; the National Art Collections Fund, Scottish Fund; the National Heritage Memorial Fund; and George Smith M.A., 1991 *ill.p. 3*

4 ***Shop and Office Block in an Arcaded Street:***
front elevation *c.* 1915
Pencil, ink and watercolour; 28.9 x 79.8; Signed
Purchased with the support of the National Fund for Acquisitions; the National Art Collections Fund, Scottish Fund; the National Heritage Memorial Fund; and George Smith M.A., 1991 *ill. p. 5*

5 ***Memorial Fountain in a Public Place:***
elevation and plans *c.* 1915
Pencil, ink and watercolour; 33.0 x 64.5; Signed
Lent by Strathclyde University Archives

6 **Street lampstandards: elevations and sections** *c.* 1915
Pencil, ink and watercolour;
a) 29.3 x 17.5 b) 29.4 x 30.5; Signed c) 29.8 x 18.3
Lent by Strathclyde University Archives

7 ***War Memorial in a Public Place:***
elevations and plan *c.* 1915
Pencil, ink and watercolour; 30.5 x 48.0; Signed
Lent by Strathclyde University Archives

8 **Office of A.E. Anderson, Architects, Northampton**
78 Derngate: proposed alterations – plans and section
1916
Pencil, ink and watercolour on prepared linen;
28.0 x 57.0
Lent by Northamptonshire Record Office

9 **a) 78 Derngate: front elevation before alteration**
c. 1915 Photograph
b) 78 Derngate: front elevation after alteration
c. 1920 Photograph

10 **78 Derngate: front door design** 1916
Pencil and watercolour on brown tracing paper;
31.1. x 20.9

11 **78 Derngate: front door design** 1916
Pencil and watercolour; 39.3 x 26.9

12 **a) 78 Derngate: rear elevation before alteration** *c.* 1915
Copy photograph from *The Ideal Home,* August 1920
ill. p. 7
b) 78 Derngate: rear elevation after alteration *c.* 1920
Photograph

13 **Studio-house for Harold Squire:**
1st stage – front elevation
Probably January-February 1920
Pencil; 28.1 x 19.5

14 **Studio-house for Harold Squire:**
2nd stage – front and rear elevations and plans
Probably March-June 1920
Pencil, ink and watercolour; 45.5 x 66.1; Signed

15 **Studio-house for Harold Squire:**
2nd stage – plan and sections
Probably March-June 1920
Pencil, ink and watercolour; 46.0 x 68.0; Signed

16 **Studio-house for Harold Squire:**
3rd stage – plans, elevations and sections
June-October 1920
Pencil, ink and watercolour on prepared linen;
45.5 x 75.0; Signed; stamped 29 October 1920

17 **Studio-house for Arthur Cadogan Blunt**
a) Plans and front and rear elevations
February-May 1920
Pencil, ink and watercolour on brown tracing
paper; 43.9 x 43.3; Signed
b) Front elevation incorporating old timbers
May 1920 or later
Pencil, ink and watercolour on cream tracing
paper; 22.2 x 21.0

18 **Studios for Francis Derwent Wood:**
1st stage – plans and sketch of rear elevation
Probably February-June 1920
Pencil, ink and watercolour on brown tracing
paper; 31.8 x 49.6

19 **Studios for Francis Derwent Wood:**
1st stage – front elevation and section
Probably February-June 1920
Pencil, ink and watercolour with crayon on brown
tracing paper; 31.6 x 49.6 *ill. p. 11*

20 ***Block of Studios:*** **studios and studio-flats for the Arts League of Service: plans, elevations and perspective in vignette**
May 1920 or later
Pencil and watercolour; 27.6 x 37.2
Lent by the Trustees of The British Museum
(1981-12-12-24) *ill. p. 12*

21 **Studios and studio-flats for the Arts League of Service:**
a) ground floor plan; b) third floor plan
May 1920 or later
Pencil, ink and watercolour on brown tracing
paper; a) 33.7 x 24.9 b) 34.0 x 24.9

22 **Studio and studio-flats for the Arts League of Service:**
sections May 1920 or later
Pencil, ink and watercolour on brown tracing
paper; 33.6 x 24.8

23 ***Three Chelsea Studios: Elevation to Glebe Place***
Probably December 1920 or later
Pencil and watercolour; 27.6 x 37.2
Lent by the Trustees of The British Museum
(1981-12-12-22) *ill. p. 11*

24 ***Three Chelsea Studios: Elevation to Cheyne House Garden*** Probably December 1920 or later
Pencil and watercolour; 27.6 x 37.2
Lent by the Trustees of The British Museum
(1981-12-12-23) *ill. p. 11*

25 **A Block of studios round a courtyard:**
front elevation *c.* 1920
Pencil and watercolour on brown paper; 42.5 x 55.7

26 **A Block of studios round a courtyard: plan** *c.* 1920
Pencil, ink and watercolour on cream tracing paper; 37.3 x 46.7

27 **Theatre for Margaret Morris**
a) Front elevation and sections 1920
Pencil, ink and watercolour; 44.0 x 72.0; Signed
ill. p.13
b) Plans 1920
Pencil, ink and watercolour; 44.5 x 72.0; Signed

28 **Studio-cottage for E.O. Hoppé: elevations and section** 1920
Pencil, ink and watercolour; 56.7 x 39.1; Signed

29 **Studio-cottage for E.O. Hoppé: plans** 1920
Pencil, ink and watercolour; 57.1 x 39.2; Signed

30 **Leigh Farm Cottages, Ansty, Sussex: proposed alterations – elevations, sections and plans** 1920-21
Pencil, ink and watercolour on white tracing paper; 46.7 x 64.1
Lent by the British Architectural Library Drawings Collection, Royal Institute of British Architects

31 **a) Design for an advertising label for W.J. Bassett-Lowke Ltd** *c.* 1921
Pencil and watercolour; 20.7 x 26.2
b) Greetings card for Mr and Mrs W.J. Bassett-Lowke 1921
Colour lithograph on white card; 9.2 x 13.9; Signed and dated *ill. p. 27*

32 **Ernest Noble**
Greetings card for W.J. Bassett-Lowke 1935
Colour lithograph; 15.2 x 10.8
Lent by Janet Bassett-Lowke

33 **a) Design for an advertising label for Bassett-Lowke Ltd** *c.* 1921
Pencil and watercolour; 26.1 x 20.6
b) Design for an advertising label for Bassett-Lowke Ltd *c.* 1921
Pencil and watercolour; 24.5 x 20.6
c) Advertising label for Bassett-Lowke Ltd *c.* 1921
Colour lithograph on white adhesive paper; 6.4 x 4.6

34 **a) Design for an advertising label for Bassett-Lowke Ltd** *c.* 1921
Pencil and watercolour; 22.9 x 20.5
b) Design for an advertising label for Bassett-Lowke Ltd *c.* 1921
Pencil and watercolour; 26.1 x 20.5
c) Advertising label for Bassett-Lowke Ltd *c.* 1921
Colour lithograph on white adhesive paper; 6.4 x 4.6

35 **Clock design 'A' for W.J. Bassett-Lowke** 1917
Pencil and watercolour; 26.4 x 20.6

36 **Clock design 'B' for W.J. Bassett-Lowke** 1917
Pencil and watercolour; 26.2 x 20.4

37 **Letters from W.J. Bassett-Lowke to C.R. Mackintosh**
a) 31 July 1916 b) 2 November 1916
c) 12 January 1917 d) 14 January 1917
Signed and dated

38 **78 Derngate: design for lounge-hall standard lamp, staircase screen and chair** 1916
Pencil and watercolour; 34.3 x 51.6

39 **78 Derngate: design for lounge-hall and stair carpets** 1916
Pencil and watercolour on brown tracing paper; 31.0 x 26.0; Signed

40 **78 Derngate: design for lounge-hall stencil** 1916
Pencil and watercolour; 80.0 x 56.5 *ill. p. 21*

41 **78 Derngate: design for lounge-hall fireplace and cabinet** 1916
Pencil and watercolour; 37.2 x 53.0

42 **78 Derngate: design for lounge-hall curtains** 1916
Pencil, ink and watercolour on brown tracing paper; 19.7 x 19.4
Purchased with the support of the National Fund for Acquisitions and the National Art Collection Fund, Scottish Fund, 1994

43 **78 Derngate: design for guest bedroom furniture and wall decoration** 1917
Pencil and watercolour; 30.5 x 76.0; Dated

44 **Candida Cottage: design for a sideboard** 1918
Pencil and watercolour; 21.5 x 39.1; Dated

45 **Candida Cottage: design for a sideboard** 1918
Pencil and watercolour; 21.6 x 39.2; Dated

46 **a) Candida Cottage: design for a sideboard, table and chair** 1918
Pencil and watercolour; 36.2 x 78.2; Dated
b) Design for tables, chairs and a sideboard 1918
Pencil and watercolour; 32.8 x 78.5; Signed

47 **Candida Cottage: design for sideboards and a gramophone cabinet** 1918
Pencil and watercolour; 20.8 x 45.8

48 **Candida Cottage: design for a service trolley, sideboard and coffee table** 1918
Pencil and watercolour; 35.9 x 47.1

49 **Schematic model of studio proposals for Francis Derwent Wood, Harold Squire and the Arts League of Service based on designs (20), (23) and (24)**
Painted MDF; 1/4" : 1'
Model by Stephen Perry, Hunterian Art Gallery

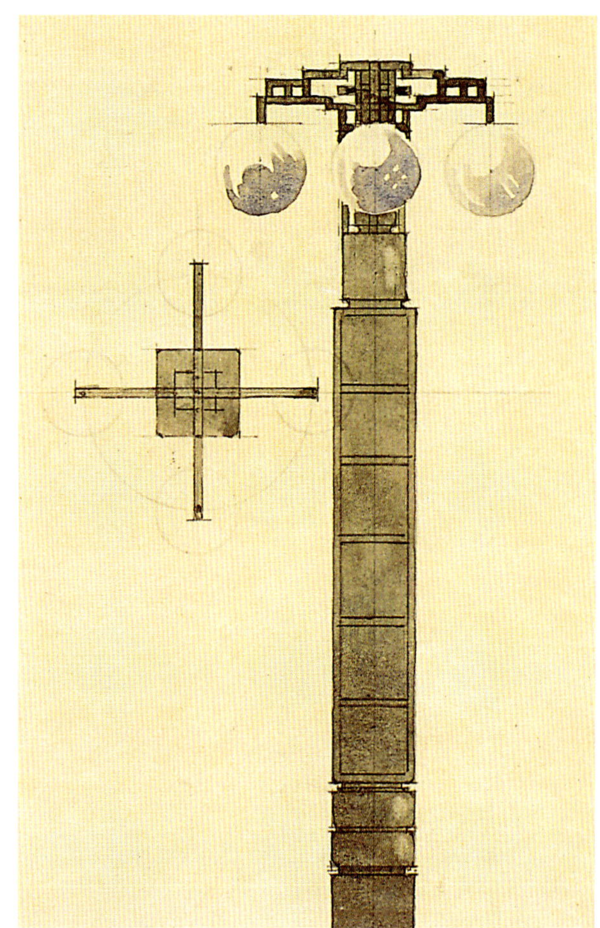

cat. 6. b - detail

Illustrations
Cover Design: based on a leaded glass panel for the lounge-hall screen, 78 Derngate.
Frontispiece: E.O. Hoppé: *C.R.Mackintosh c.* 1920.
Lost and Found: ill. 6 photo by R. Inglis pre-1914 from John Bignell *Chelsea seen from its earliest days* (London 1987); ills. 7, 8 and 10 © The Trustees of the British Museum; ill. 12 photo courtesy Alan Crawford, © Anthony Kersting.
A Memoir of W.J. Bassett-Lowke: ill. 1 courtesy Janet Bassett-Lowke; ill. 5 photo courtesy Northamptonshire Record Office from Rolland Fuller *The Bassett-Lowke Story* (London 1984); ill. 7 ex-coll. the late Colin Robinson; ill. 8 photo courtesy Alan Burman; ill. 10 from *The Architectural Review* 1926, © Glasgow City Libraries, The Mitchell Library
Other photographs were provided by Glasgow University Media Services (Photographic)

ISBN 0-904254-62-3